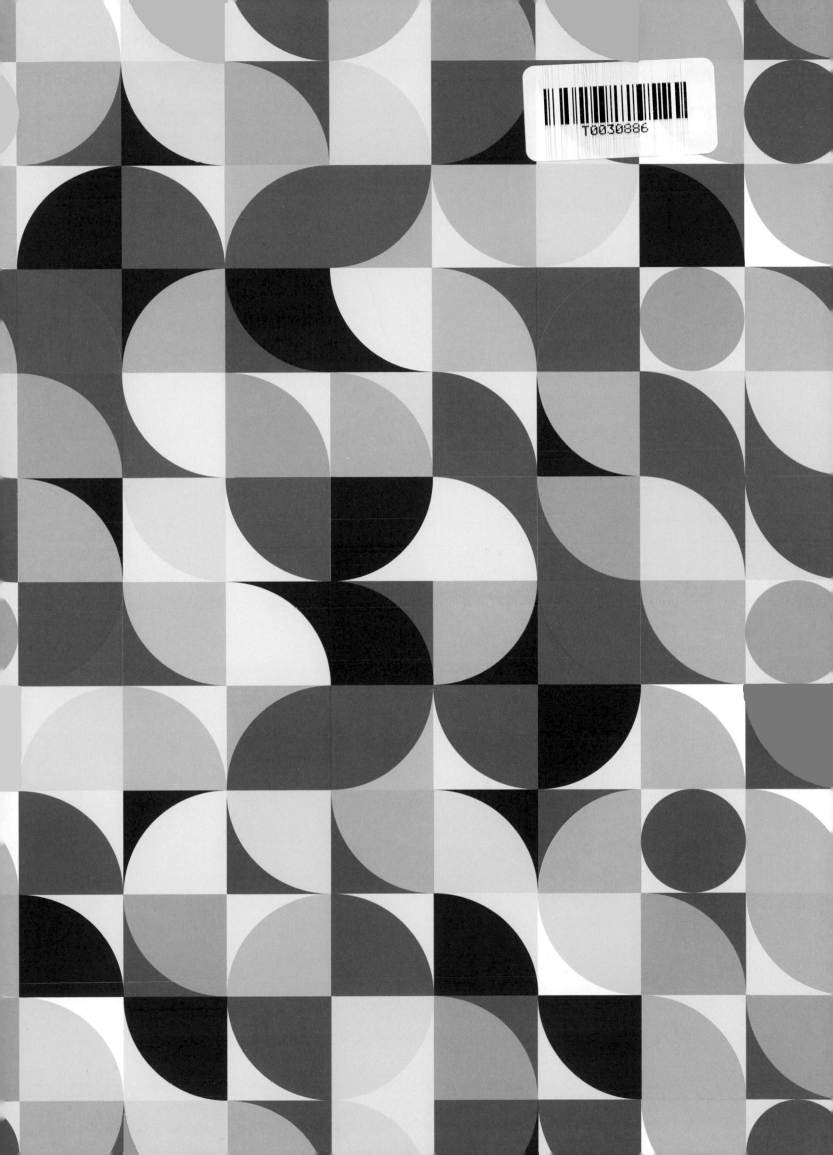

To my children—Kirsten, Robin, Laura, Rebekah, Christian, and Rachel—who taught me about loving-kindness. —C. M.

Text copyright © 2024 by Christy Monson
Illustrations copyright © 2024 by Teresa Bellón

Published by Bushel & Peck Books, a family-run publishing house in Fresno, California, who believes in uplifting children with the highest standards of art, music, literature, and ideas. For every book we sell, we donate one to a child in need—book for book. To nominate a school or organization to receive free books, or to find inspiring books and gifts, please visit www.bushelandpeckbooks.com.

LCCN: 2024931202
ISBN: 978-1-63819-095-0

First Edition

Printed in China

1 3 5 7 9 10 8 6 4 2

Mindful
Magic

23
Meditations
for Calm Kids

CHRISTY MONSON, LMFT

Illustrated by TERESA BELLÓN

BUSHEL
& PECK
BOOKS

Contents

Introduction

Children lead increasingly busy lives today, making it important for them to take some time to find calm in their daily routine. School, media, and other activities bombard children in ways that pull them from the focus necessary for a peaceful life. Tranquility can escape all of us if we let our lives and the lives of our children be buffeted about by daily happenings. Fortunately, mindfulness and visualization techniques can help restore peace, even for kids!

MINDFULNESS

Mindfulness, the art of being present in the moment, can bring calm to our demanding existence. As we concentrate on our breathing and are aware of each present moment, we find tranquility and focus. Some of the benefits of mindfulness include increased positive emotions, better sleep patterns, less anxiety, less depression, and less emotional reactivity.

VISUALIZATION

Visualization is another powerful tool that can invite calm. Thinking creates our feelings. As children tap into the ability to use their thinking, along with visualization, to regulate their feelings, their quality of life improves. They will move from a place of letting their emotions control them to being able to choose their feelings.

Some of the exercises in this book are designed to help kids find the magic of their imaginations. As they tap into thoughts, visualizations, and artistic ideas, they will enhance their creativity, and the undreamed-of can become reality in their lives. In addition, the visualization exercises in the Connection Section will help the entire family focus on kindness, positive self-esteem, and a relationship with loved ones.

HOW TO USE THIS BOOK

This book contains twenty-three mindfulness and visualization meditations, which you can practice along with your kids, grandkids, or students. Let your inner child enjoy them as well! No matter the nature of each meditation, every exercise ends with a deep breath in and a gentle breath out, the core of all mindfulness techniques. How you use each meditation is up to you. You might find that one time through a meditation is enough to ground your child, or you may find that repeating the meditation (or a portion of it) several times is helpful. Or, you might also do several different meditations in a row, instead. You can do these exercises anywhere—in the car, at home, on a trip, in the classroom, or even on the playground at school. You might schedule a time and practice them regularly each morning, do one before bedtime to invite better sleep, try a meditation to unwind after a stressful day at school, or just keep the book handy for tough times when your child needs calm in a pinch. Some meditations will work better for your child than others, and that's okay! Come back to your favorites again and again, and watch as mindfulness becomes truly magical for both of you.

Nature's
Peace

Does your mind jump around sometimes, like a leaf blowing in the wind? It's hard to concentrate if your mind is tumbling about in the breeze. Here are a few exercises to help you slow down and find a calm place inside you. Before you start, find a comfortable place. Sit up straight (but not rigid) and hold your body gently still. You could also stretch out on your bed if you prefer. Take a deep breath in, clear down into your belly. Then breathe out gently. Ready? Let's try Nature's Peace.

Blow a Feather

- Close your eyes and cup your hand, as if you're cradling a soft, downy feather.
- Hold the feather carefully between your thumb and finger.
- Take a deep breath in.
- Now breathe out ever so lightly, just enough to wiggle the plumes.
- Take another deep breath in and blow out gently, wiggling the plumes again.
- ♥ Blow another feather until you feel calm.

Apple Blossom Snow

- Close your eyes an imagine you are sitting under an apple tree with blossoms falling all around you.
- Notice each and every blossom as they gently drift in the air. They are white with pink edges and yellow stamens in the middle. Each petal floats to the ground like snow.
- Scoop up the blossoms near you in your hands.
- Take a deep breath in and smell the sweet scent all around you.
- Breathe out gently, blowing the petals away and letting them flutter to the ground. You're making magical springtime snow.
- ♥ Scoop up more blossoms and blow again.

Flower Power

- Close your eyes and imagine wrapping yourself in field of lavender.
- Breathe in through your nose and out through your mouth, smelling the flowers and letting the soft fragrance tickle your nose.
- Take a deep breath in and breathe out gently.
- Feel the scent travel through your entire body. Lavender relaxes and calms.
- Take a deep breath in and breathe out gently.
- Smell the lavender until you feel calm.

Watching the Waves

- Close your eyes and imagine ocean waves lapping the shore.
- Watch the water rush in and out, in and out.
- Watch the white foam on each wave fizzle away.
- Take a deep breath in and breathe out gently.
- Take another breath in, smelling the salty ocean.
- Breathe out, feeling the cool ocean mist brush your face.
- Wiggle your toes like they're in the soft mushy sand.
- Listen to the water rush back to the ocean.
- Take a deep breath in and breathe out gently.
- ♥ Listen to the waves until you feel calm.

Whispering Forest

- Stand on the ground, close your eyes, and imagine you are a tall tree in the forest.
- Feel your feet firmly touching the ground. Imagine you have roots deep in the soil that keep you solid. There are trees all around to steady you.
- Lift your arms and sway gently, imagining a gentle breeze blowing your top branches back and forth, back and forth.
- Lower your arms and take a deep breath in and breathe out gently.
- In your mind, picture the greens and browns and plants and animals of the forest around you.
- Smell the fragrant pines in your nose.
- Hear the singing birds in your ears.
- Feel a cool gust of air brush your skin.
- Feel afternoon sunshine warming your face and neck.
- Take a deep breath in and breathe out gently.
- Listen to the breeze whisper:
    - "I am strong."
    - "I matter."
    - "I believe in myself."
- Take a deep breath in and breathe out gently.
- ♥ Listen to the breeze until you feel calm.

Focus with Color

Sometimes it's hard to keep our minds fixed on our daily tasks. Inside our heads, our attention can jump from one thought to another. Outside our heads, we can get distracted by noises and people around us. But we can teach our minds to focus. We can learn to concentrate on things we need to do. With practice, our minds will get better and better at paying attention. Here are some exercises to help you focus. Before you start, find a comfortable place, sit up straight, and breathe deeply. Now let's Focus with Color.

The Strong, Red Lighthouse

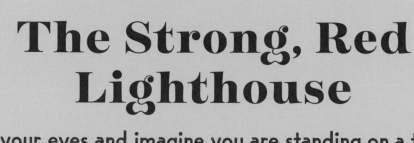

- Close your eyes and imagine you are standing on a tall hill by a red lighthouse.
- Take a deep breath in and breathe out gently.
- Climb the lighthouse steps, moving your feet with each step, until you reach the top deck.
- The ocean stretches before you. Stand by the red railing and watch white foamy waves crash against the rocks below.
- Breathe in the power of the blue ocean as giant waves dash the gray cliff.
- Breathe out gently.
- The white spray shoots upward, reaching for you and for the blue sky. Breathe in its strength.
- Breathe out gently.
- ♥ Continue until you feel calm.

The Tireless, Gray Seagull

- Close your eyes and imagine you are a gray and white seagull flying over a deep, blue ocean.
- Take a deep breath in and breathe out gently.
- Put out your arms like wings and imagine you are soaring through the air. Fly through a spray of white mist and up, up into the blue sky.
- Circle around back into the spray. You feel the water mist your wings.
- Take a deep breath in and breathe out gently. Water is energy.
- Soar high and say to yourself,

    "I am strength."

    "I can conquer."

    "I am power."

- Take a deep breath in and breathe out gently.
- ♥ Soar high again until you feel calm.

The Focused Blue Lake

- Close your eyes and imagine you are near a quiet, deep-blue lake.
- Take a deep breath in and breathe out gently.
- Listen to the stillness.
- Pick up a small, smooth pebble with your hand and toss it into the lake.
- Watch the rings of water grow outward, one after the other, until they finally disappear.
- Take a deep breath in and breathe out gently.
- Drop another peble and watch the rings until you feel calm.

The Determined Yellow Sun

- Close your eyes and picture a bright yellow sun shining overhead, smiling down on a tree heavy with oranges.
- Take a deep breath in and breathe out gently.
- Reach out your hand and pluck an orange from the tree.
- Cup the orange in your hand. You feel the warmth of the orange as it rests heavy in your hand.
- Peel the orange and bite into its bursting flavor. Slurp up the juice. Yellow sunshine and orange flavor fill you with happy energy and determination. You can do anything!
- Take a deep breath in and breathe out gently.

Artful Imagination

Your imagination is a special part of you. You can design anything you want in your mind. You can visit special places. Create a secret retreat each day by spending time in your imagination. Art is a great way to share your feelings, and you can invent mind-pictures anywhere and anytime because your imagination is always with you. It's the best brain exercise ever. Stretch out in a comfy place in your bedroom or under a shady tree. Now, give your mind an Artful Imagination workout.

Squiggle Drawing

Picture a large white sheet of paper in your mind.

Imagine picking up your favorite color and drawing a squiggle on the paper.

Take a deep breath in and breathe out gently.

Turn the paper all around and get to know your squiggle.

Expand your squiggle into a drawing of your favorite place.

Fill in the colors with your mind.

Take a deep breath in and breathe out gently.

Breathe in everything about your favorite place. What scents do you smell? What foods do you taste? What sounds do you hear? What do you like best about your place?

Take a deep breath in and breathe out gently.

♥ Enjoy your favorite place for as long as you wish.

Building Blocks

- Close your eyes and picture a pile of soft, foam building blocks. Notice all the different shapes and colors. Red, orange, yellow, green, and blue. Squares, triangles, circles, rectangles, and ovals.
- Reach out your fingers and pinch their soft squishiness.
- Take a deep breath in and breathe out gently.
- Now, think of something you want to build. A tall building? A fancy park? A train or an airplane?
- Take a deep breath in and breathe out gently.
- Create your building idea. Picture each block softly fitting into place.
- Take a deep breath in and breathe out gently.
- Work on your building for as long as you wish. When you're finished, gently knock it over and let each block tumble softly to the ground.
- Take a deep breath in and breathe out gently.
- ♥ Make more creations if you wish.

Nature Songs

- Close your eyes and imagine you're resting on a mountain path by a tumbling stream. The water gurgles and splashes over the rocks on its way down the hill.

- Take a deep breath in and breathe out gently.

- Listen to the song the water creates. Can you hum a tune like it in your head?

- Take a deep breath in and breathe out gently.

- There are birds in the trees overhead, singing to greet the day.

- Listen to the blue bird. What song is she singing? Can you hum a tune like it in your head?

- Now the cardinal. What song is he singing? Can you hum a tune like it in your head?

- Now listen to the robin. Hum a tune to greet the day just like he does.

- Take a deep breath in and breathe out gently.
- There's a mother squirrel chattering to her babies in a nearby tree. You listen, and you realize she's speaking to you, too. She says:

  "You are safe."

  "You are important."

  "You have a place in this world."
- Take a deep breath in and breathe out gently.
- ♥ Listen for more sounds if you wish.

Animal Antics

Do you ever feel bored? Like you have no energy? A case of the blaahhs? Or maybe you have the wiggles inside you that just won't go away. Your imagination can call you from boredom and from wiggles. Before you begin, stand tall and take a deep breath that fills you clear down to your belly. Let it slowly out. Let's give those blaahhs and wiggles something to do with some Animal Antics!

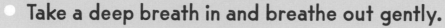

Monkey Face

- Take a deep breath in and breathe out gently.
- Put on your monkey face.
- Squeeze your lips together and make a monkey-kissing sound.
- Wiggle your monkey ears.
- Raise your monkey eyebrows up and down.
- Stick out your monkey tongue.
- Take a deep monkey breath in and breathe out your monkey breath gently.
- Touch your monkey nose with your finger.
- Turn your monkey head to the left. Now turn your monkey head to the right.
- Take a deep monkey breath in and breathe out your monkey breath gently.
- ♥ Create more antics if you wish.

Slithering Snake

- Close your eyes and imagine a snake is slithering up your arms. Its cool smoothness glides along your skin.
- Take a deep snake breath in and hiss your snake breath out gently.
- The snake slips across your shoulders, tickling your back as it twists along.
- Take a deep snake breath in and hiss your snake breath out gently.
- The snake turns its head and nods to you as it winds down your other arm and off your hand.
- Take a deep snake breath in and hiss your snake breath out gently. Good-bye, snake.
- ♥ Slither more antics if you wish.

Gliding Manta Ray

- Take a deep breath in and breathe out gently.
- Hold your arms out like the triangle arms of a gliding manta ray.
- Wave your arms gently to one side and then the other.
- Take a deep breath in and breathe out gently.
- Dip your body to one side and then the other. The manta ray is peaceful. Can you feel its peace?
- ♥ Take a deep breath in and breathe out gently.

Alligator Snap

Take a deep breath in and breathe out gently.

Hold your arms together in front of you like alligator jaws.

Lift one arm up and the other arm down. Count, "One . . . two . . . three . . ."

Wiggle your fingers like an alligator-tongue, looking for food.

Snap your arms together tight. Did you find any food?

Take a deep breath in and breathe out gently.

Lift one arm up and the other arm down. Count, "One . . . two . . . three . . ."

Wiggle your fingers like an alligator tongue, looking for food.

Snap your arms together tight. You found yummy food.

Take a deep breath in and breathe out gently.

♥ Your tummy is full. Make an alligator smile.

Baby Elephant Trot

- Sit tall in your chair, close your eyes, and imagine you're a baby elephant.
- Tap your baby elephant feet on the floor, trotting to catch up with your mother.
- Take in short breaths until you are by her side.
- Let your breath out gently as you hold your arms together and wave them like a trunk.
- Smell the earth as your trunk snuffles the ground.
- Trot your feet on the floor to catch your mother again.
- Take in short breaths until you are by her side.
- Let your breath out gently as you hold your arms together and wave them like a trunk.
- Smell the muddy earth as your trunk snuffles the ground.
- Your mother has stopped at the watering hole for a drink. Dip your trunk arms into the water and drink with a slurping noise.
- Your belly is full of water and your mother gives you a trunk hug. Trunk hug her back.
- Take a deep breath in and breathe out gently.
- ♥ Hug until you feel calm.

Connection Section

Spending time with family and being with friends is something we all love to do. Sometimes family members do kind things for us, like fixing delicious dinners or reading stories before tucking us into bed. And sometimes we do nice things for them as well, like picking up our toys or playing with the baby for a few minutes. We all feel good when we do thoughtful things for others. Connection Section will help you connect with the loved ones in your life.

Loving Others

AS WE PRACTICE DOING KIND THINGS, WE GET BETTER AND BETTER AT IT. WE FEEL HAPPY INSIDE WHEN WE HELP THOSE AROUND US.

- Close your eyes.
- Take a deep breath in and breathe out gently.
- Picture a good deed you did today. Feelings of light and love come when we help others. Let these fillings fill you up.
- Take a deep breath in and breathe out gently.
- Now picture a kindness you haven't done yet today, but you will do. What will it be?
- Take a deep breath in and breathe out gently.
- ♥ Open your eyes and do your next kind deed. Notice as light and love fill you up again!

Self-Connection

WE ALL MAKE MISTAKES AND MESS THINGS UP SOMETIMES. ARE YOU ANGRY WITH YOURSELF WHEN THAT HAPPENS? THINK OF THE LAST TIME YOU MADE A MISTAKE. WERE YOU NICE TO YOURSELF? WHAT DOES KINDNESS FOR YOURSELF MEAN? BE AS GOOD TO YOURSELF AS YOU ARE TO OTHERS. REMEMBER EVERYONE MAKES MISTAKES, EVEN YOUR FRIENDS AND PARENTS.

- Close your eyes.
- Take a deep breath in and breathe out gently.
- Put your hands over your heart and give yourself a heart hug.
- Say out loud:

  "It's okay to try again."

  "Nobody's perfect."

- Take a deep breath in and breathe out gently.
- Wrap your arms around yourself in a hug and say out loud:

  "I made a mistake, but I'm not a mistake."

  "I learn from my mess-ups."

  "I love myself."

  "I get better and better each day."

- Take a deep breath in and breathe out gently.
- Continue until you feel better about yourself.

Thought Connections

- Close your eyes.
- Take a deep breath in and breathe out gently.
- Picture three good things you did today. Maybe you did well on a spelling test. Maybe you sat by a new kid at lunch. Maybe you hugged your mom.
- Take a deep breath in and breathe out gently.
- Name your three good things aloud and give yourself a pat on the back each time.
- Now, picture three ways that other people helped you today. Maybe someone waved to you on the playground. Maybe your dog wagged his tail at you. Maybe Mom made your favorite cookies.
- Say, "Thank you," and name each person aloud.
- Take a deep breath in and breathe out gently.
- ♥ Create more thought connections if you wish.

Far-Away Connections

SOMETIMES WE HAVE FAMILY, TEACHERS, AND FRIENDS THAT LIVE FAR AWAY FROM US. MAYBE YOU AND YOUR FAMILY MOVED TO A NEW PLACE, AND YOU LEFT LOVED ONES AND FRIENDS BEHIND. YOU AND YOUR FAR-AWAY PERSON CAN BE TOGETHER ANYTIME. IMAGINATION IS A GREAT WAY TO SHARE. YOU MIGHT ENCOURAGE THEM TO HAVE IMAGINATION MEETINGS TOO!

- Close your eyes.
- Take a deep breath in and breathe out gently.
- Picture a favorite far-away person.
- Now imagine walking with them to the park.
- Link arms and tell them how much you love and miss them. Share the wonderful things about your new home and discuss the hard things also.
- Take a deep breath in and breathe out gently.
- Remember a favorite joke to share. Laugh together.
- Say, "I'll see you next time."
- Take a deep breath in and breathe out gently.
- ♥ Repeat whenever you'd like to be with your friend.

Family Connections

DO YOU HAVE FAMILY MEMBERS THAT ARE NO LONGER WITH YOU? MAYBE THEY PASSED AWAY FROM AN ILLNESS OR DIED FROM OLD AGE. YOU REMEMBER THEM AND MISS THEM. MAYBE YOU FEEL LONELY WITHOUT THEM AND WANT TO TALK TO THEM LIKE YOU USED TO. THEY CAN STILL BE WITH YOU. MEET THEM IN YOUR IMAGINATION.

- Close your eyes, take a deep breath in, and breathe out gently.
- Imagine the family member you miss and bring them to a favorite place you both loved in your mind.
- Tell them you miss them and curl up on their lap if you choose.
- Share the things you've been doing.
- Take a deep breath in and breathe out gently.
- Let them know your problems.
- Tell them your solutions and ask for their suggestions.
- Think about their ideas and discuss them.
- Take a deep breath in and breathe out gently.
- ♥ They are part of you, and you are part of them. Enjoy time together whenever you want.

Gratitude Meditation

- Close your eyes, take a deep breath in, and breathe out gently.
- Let your arms rest against the chair.
- Say, "Thank you, arms, for all the good things you do for me."
- Touch your feet to the floor.
- Say, "Thank you, feet, for helping me run and jump."
- Take a deep breath in and breathe out gently.
- Say, "Thank you, air, for breath."
- Take a deep breath in and breathe out gently.
- Hear loved ones talking somewhere nearby.
- Say, "Thank you, friends, for loving me."
- Take a deep breath in and breathe out gently.
- Sense the sun, moon, or stars shining through your window.
- Say, "Thank you, sun, moon, and stars, for sharing your light."
- You are an important part of the world and the universe.
- Say, "Thank you, world and universe, for a place to live."
- Take a deep breath in and breathe out gently.
- ♥ Think of other things you are grateful for.

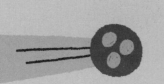

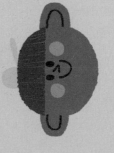

About Bushel & Peck

Bushel & Peck Books is a children's publishing house with a special mission. Through our Book-for-Book Promise™, we donate one book to kids in need for every book we sell. Our beautiful books are given to kids through schools, libraries, local neighborhoods, shelters, nonprofits, and also to many selfless organizations who are working hard to make a difference. So thank you for purchasing this book! Because of you, another book will find its way into the hands of a child who needs it most.